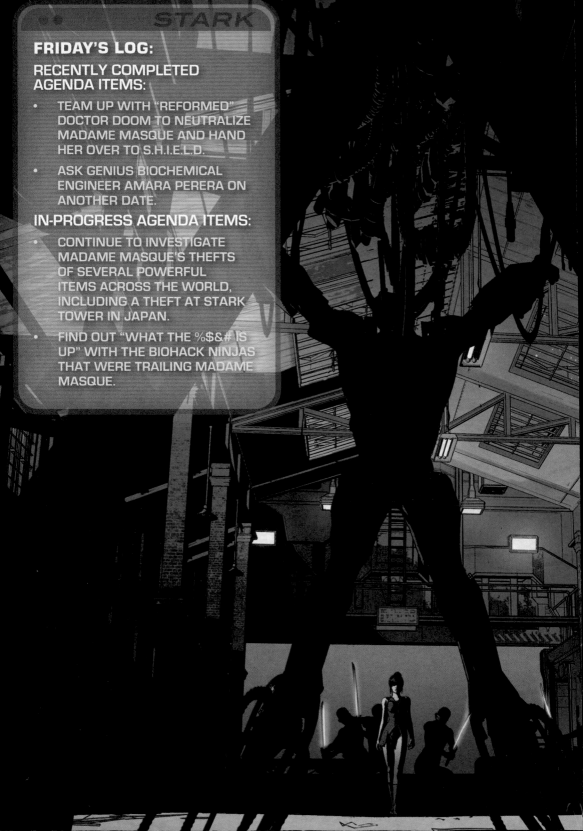

FRIDAY'S LOG:

RECENTLY COMPLETED
AGENDA ITEMS:

- TEAM UP WITH "REFORMED"
DOCTOR DOOM TO NEUTRALIZE
MADAME MASQUE AND HAND
HER OVER TO S.H.I.E.L.D.

- ASK GENIUS BIOCHEMICAL
ENGINEER AMARA PERERA ON
ANOTHER DATE.

IN-PROGRESS AGENDA ITEMS:

- CONTINUE TO INVESTIGATE
MADAME MASQUE'S THEFTS
OF SEVERAL POWERFUL
ITEMS ACROSS THE WORLD,
INCLUDING A THEFT AT STARK
TOWER IN JAPAN.

- FIND OUT "WHAT THE %$&# IS
UP" WITH THE BIOHACK NINJAS
THAT WERE TRAILING MADAME
MASQUE.

...LIONAIRE PLAYBOY AND GENIUS INDUSTRIALIST TONY STARK WAS KIDNAPPED DURING A ROUTINE WEAPONS TEST. HIS ...PTORS ATTEMPTED TO FORCE HIM TO BUILD A WEAPON OF MASS DESTRUCTION. INSTEAD HE CREATED A POWERED SUIT OF ARMOR THAT SAVED HIS LIFE. FROM THAT DAY ON, HE USED THE SUIT TO PROTECT THE WORLD AS THE...

INVINCIBLE
IRON MAN

THE WAR MACHINES

BRIAN MICHAEL BENDIS
WRITER

MIKE DEODATO
ARTIST

FRANK MARTIN
COLOR ARTIST

VC'S CLAYTON COWLES
LETTERER

MIKE DEODATO (#6-9, #11) WITH
FRANK MARTIN (#6, #8-9),
DEAN WHITE (#7) &
RAIN BEREDO (#11)
AND
KATE NIEMCZYK (#10)
COVER ART

ALANNA SMITH
ASSISTANT EDITOR

TOM BREVOORT
EDITOR

IRON MAN CREATED BY STAN LEE, LARRY LIEBER, DON HECK & JACK KIRBY

COLLECTION EDITOR: **JENNIFER GRÜNWALD**
ASSOCIATE EDITOR: **SARAH BRUNSTAD**
ASSOCIATE MANAGING EDITOR: **ALEX STARBUCK**
EDITOR, SPECIAL PROJECTS: **MARK D. BEAZLEY**
VP, PRODUCTION & SPECIAL PROJECTS: **JEFF YOUNGQUIST**
SVP PRINT, SALES & MARKETING: **DAVID GABRIEL**
BOOK DESIGNER: **JAY BOWEN**

EDITOR IN CHIEF: **AXEL ALONSO**
CHIEF CREATIVE OFFICER: **JOE QUESADA**
PUBLISHER: **DAN BUCKLEY**
EXECUTIVE PRODUCER: **ALAN FINE**

VINCIBLE IRON MAN VOL. 2: THE WAR MACHINES. Contains material originally published in magazine form as INVINCIBLE IRON MAN #6-11. First printing 2016. ISBN# 978-0-7851-9521-4. Published by MARVEL WORLDWIDE, INC., a
sidiary of MARVEL ENTERTAINMENT, LLC. OFFICE OF PUBLICATION: 135 West 50th Street, New York, NY 10020. Copyright © 2016 MARVEL. No similarity between any of the names, characters, persons, and/or institutions in this magazine

STARK

BROADCASTING LIVE FROM...

STARK TOWER, OSAKA, JAPAN.

FRIDAY?

YES?

LET ME GET THIS STRAIGHT-- MADAME MASQUE USED THIS WINDOW AS HER EXIT?

SHE COULDN'T USE ANY OF THE DOORS?

THAT IS A BIG YES.

IT WOULD SEEM SHE WAS IN A HURRY.

AND WE STILL DON'T KNOW WHAT SHE STOLE?

THERE IS NOTHING MISSING IN THE BUILDING'S PERSONAL OR BUSINESS INVENTORY.

WHAT DOES THE SECURITY FOOTAGE SHOW?

THAT SHE HAD SOME WAY TO HIDE HER MOVEMENTS. SHE SCRAMBLED THE SYSTEM AS SHE WENT.

WE ONLY HAVE BITS AND PIECES.

SHOW ME THE BITS AND PIECES...

THAT'S IT?

THAT'S IT.

I'M GOING INSIDE.

YOU SCANNING THE ROOM FOR ME, FRIDAY?

FULL ENVIRONMENTAL SCAN.

I'M PICKING UP VERY THIN TRACES OF ENERGY SIGNATURE RESIDUE THAT MATCHES THE BIOHACK NINJAS FROM THE BEACH ATTACK THE OTHER NIGHT.

CAN YOU TRACE IT?

NOT ENOUGH TO TRACE.

I COULD MATCH IT IF I EVER CAME ACROSS IT AGAIN.

AND THERE WERE HOW MANY OF THESE--?

<WHO ARE YOU?>*

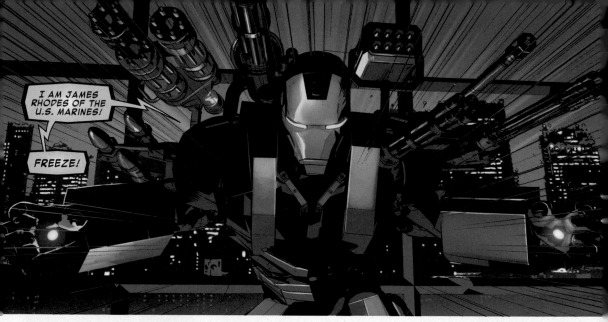

I CLEARLY LOOK AT OUR RELATIONSHIP VERY DIFFERENTLY.

MY QUESTION IS, DON'T YOU HAVE SATELLITES AND ALL KINDS OF SECURITY STUFF HERE THAT YOU SHOULD BE GOING OVER INSTEAD OF HAVING ME SCARE THAT POOR WOMAN?

IT'S THE SAME REASON ENGLAND STILL HAS JAMES BOND.

SOMETIMES YOU JUST NEED A REAL PERSON IN THE FIELD LOOKING FOR CLUES.

YOU KNOW JAMES BOND ISN'T A REAL PERSON, RIGHT?

I DON'T KNOW WHAT YOU'RE TALKING ABOUT.

SO AS FAR AS YOU'RE CONCERNED, YOU HAD NOTHING IN THIS BUILDING THAT WOULD BE OF SIGNIFICANT VALUE TO SOMEONE LIKE CRAZY WHITNEY FROST?

NOPE.

NOTHING THAT WAS WORTH HER BREAKING IN HERE?

NOPE.

AND NOTHING WORTH BEING CHASED OUT BY SOME NEW NEXT-LEVEL NINJA PEOPLE?

YOU CAN ASK ME THREE MORE TIMES, BUBULA, BUT I DON'T KNOW WHAT SHE TOOK OR WHY SHE TOOK IT.

ALL I KNOW IS THAT SHE WAS DABBLING IN SOME DEMONIC FORCES--

I HATE THOSE.

AND I CERTAINLY DON'T HAVE ANYTHING IN MY POSSESSION THAT HELPS YOU DABBLE IN DEMONIC FORCES.

IT WOULD EXPLAIN A LOT ABOUT YOUR PERSONALITY IF YOU DID.

I DON'T EVEN KNOW HOW SHE WAS ABLE TO MANIPULATE THE SECURITY FOOTAGE LIKE THAT.

BUT THAT COULD HAVE BEEN DEMONIC STUFF AS WELL.

I'M REALLY NOT A BIG FAN OF MYSTICISM AND DEMONIC POSSESSION.

WELL, IT AIN'T LIKE THERE'S A LOT OF PEOPLE WHO ARE.

EXACTLY. I LIKE SCIENCE. I LIKE MATH.

I'M GOING TO SNIFF AROUND THE CITY AND SEE WHAT I CAN FIND.

THAT IS A WONDERFUL GESTURE ON YOUR PART.

BUT IT IN NO WAY RELIEVES YOU OF THE DEBT YOU OWE ME FOR THE REST OF YOUR LIFE.

DO I GET TO KEEP FRIDAY?

SHE'S AN ARTIFICIAL INTELLIGENCE SMARTER THAN BOTH OF

SOME CRAPPY HOLE-IN-THE-WALL DINER THAT TONY HAS RANDOMLY DECIDED HAS THE BEST WAFFLES IN THE WORLD AND THINKS IT'S CUTE TO BE THIS RICH AND EAT HERE.

THIS IS THE BEST WAFFLE I HAVE EVER HAD.

SEE?

AND I'M NOT EVEN THAT RICH ANYMORE.

HOW'S YOUR WORK COMING?

MINE IS FRUSTRATING THE HELL OUT OF ME. LET'S TALK ABOUT YOURS.

WELL, WE'RE IN THAT WEIRD TESTING PHASE.

WE'VE REVERSED SOME OF THE SYMPTOMS OF ALZHEIMER'S DISEASE IN MICE USING MAGNETIC RESONANCE.

IMAGING-GUIDED FOCUSED ULTRASOUND.

YES! THE MICE WE'RE TESTING ON--

GOD BLESS MICE.

THE TREATMENT LED TO IMPROVEMENTS IN COGNITION AND SPATIAL LEARNING IN THE TRANSGENIC MICE, BUT--

YOU DON'T WANT TO SLOW IT... YOU WANT TO SMASH ALZHEIMER'S IN THE FACE.

I WANT TO KILL IT WITH A SPEAR.

GOOD. PLEASE DO.

I'M TOTALLY SURE I'M GOING TO HAVE IT, SO...

I JUST NEED TO GET TO THE NEXT LEVEL, YOU KNOW?

OSAKA, JAPAN.

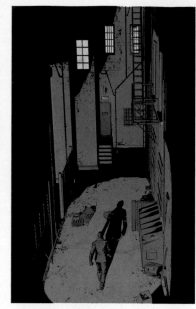

YUKIO.

NO ARMOR?

IT'S NEARBY. IT'S ALWAYS NEARBY.

ARE YOU ALONE OR--?

NO AVENGERS. NO U.S. ARMY. JUST ME.

YOU CAN SEE WHY YOUR PRESENCE HERE WOULD BE A LITTLE OFF-PUTTING.

SURE.

BUT I DON'T CARE ABOUT ANY OF YOUR ILLICIT ACTIVITIES DOWN HERE.

WHAT DO YOU CARE ABOUT?

FOR LACK OF A BETTER TERM...

...TECH-BASED NINJAS.

KUSO...

THIS IS ONE OF THOSE CONUNDRUMS.

IF I SPILL... THEY CAN *REALLY* HURT MY NEW BUSINESS.

BUT IF YOU DON'T, I HAVE ABOUT NINETY AVENGERS TEAMS THAT WOULD *LOVE* TO COME DOWN HERE AND STEP ON THIS PLACE.

I MEAN, LIKE A BIG, GIANT FOOT ACTUALLY STEPPING ON *ALL* OF THIS.

NOT HERE.

NOT HERE AS IN...?

THERE'S SOMEONE HERE RIGHT NOW?

YOU CAN'T FIGHT AND CHASE HIM HERE.

HOW LONG HAVE YOU KNOWN ABOUT THIS PLACE?

HIM WHO?

VERY BIG BOY IN THE FAR CORNER.

THAT *IS* A BIG BOY.

INHUMAN? MUTANT?

YOU KNOW, I'VE STOPPED ASKING.

WHAT DOES HE WANT?

YOU KNOW, I'VE STOPPED ASKING.

I WANT TO PROVE MY INTENTIONS TO YOUR NEW BOYFRIEND.

HE DOESN'T BELIEVE THAT I HAVE CHANGED PATHS.

YOU'VE ALREADY PHYSICALLY ATTACKED ME.

YOU KNOW I HAVE THE MYSTICAL ABILITY TO COUNTER YOUR ATTACK.

SO WHY GO THROUGH THE CHARADE OF POINTING A GUN AT ME?

YOU KEEP SNEAKING UP ON ME!

IF I CALLED YOU ON THE PHONE, WOULD YOU PICK UP?

NO.

WHAT PATH ARE YOU ON?

AMARA, PLEASE GO.

TONY, HAVE YOU HAD ANY UNUSUAL INTERACTIONS?

YES. YOU. RIGHT NOW.

NO. I MEAN, OTHERWORLDLY. UNEXPLAINABLE.

YES. YOU. RIGHT NOW.

MR. STARK AND I STOPPED A DEMONIC INTRUSION INTO OUR DIMENSION.

SOMETIMES DEMONS CAN BE PETTY AND TRY TO INFLICT PUNISHMENT DIRECTLY ON THE LIVES OF THOSE WHO WOULD STAND IN THEIR WAY.

SOMETIMES NOT.

I'M JUST TRYING TO MAKE SURE WE ARE IN THE CLEAR.

DEMONS?

FOR LACK OF A BETTER WORD.

CREATURES, REALLY.

ANIMALS WITH AN OVERBLOWN SENSE OF THEIR OWN SELF-WORTH.

THIS HAPPENED?

AMARA, I WOULD FEEL MUCH BETTER IF YOU LEFT.

I WANT TO HEAR THIS.

OTHER DIMENSIONS?

ANY UNUSUAL INTERACTIONS, STARK?

NO. I HAVE HAD NO UNUSUAL INTERACTIONS.

ANY WEIRD DREAMS?

DEFINE WEIRD...

THEY CAN COME AT YOU THROUGH YOUR DREAMS?

SLEEP IS WHEN THE HUMAN MIND IS THE MOST VULNERABLE.

I AM ATTEMPTING TO REVERSE SOME OF THE DAMAGE I HAVE INFLICTED ON--

YOU COULD SAVE THE WORLD FROM GALACTUS, THANOS AND A.T.M. CHARGES AND IT *STILL* WOULDN'T MAKE UP FOR ALL THE $%#$% YOU'VE DONE IN YOUR LIFE, DOOM.

IT WOULDN'T CHANGE ONE THING.

THIS TIME OR THE LAST.

NEXT TIME I TURN AROUND AND YOU'RE STANDING THERE... WE'RE GOING TO HAVE IT OUT.

TO THE END.

HOW ARE YOU TRACKING ME?

I'M SMARTER THAN YOU.

YOU KNOW THAT.

OF COURSE IT WOULD.

STOP DOING THIS.

STOP FOLLOWING ME. YOU'RE GOING TO FORCE ME TO--

YOU SEE THAT, ONCE AGAIN, I HAVE NOT HARMED YOU.

THIS TIME.

I JUST WANTED TO MAKE SURE YOU WERE OKAY AFTER THE LAST ENCOUNTER.

FOLLOW-UP IS NOT SOMETHING YOU SUPER HEROES ARE VERY GOOD AT.

GO TO HELL.

IT WAS LOVELY TO MEET YOU, DOCTOR.

HUMAN TESTING. IT IS YOUR NEXT PHASE.

ANYTHING ELSE IS A WASTE OF TIME.

AND IRON MAN.

invincible
IRON MAN

7

STARK.

SHARES (NASDAQ:STRK) WERE DOWN 14% AT 2:30 P.M. THURSDAY...

SETTING FRESH MULTI-YEAR LOWS DURING THE TRADING SESSION.

GOOD MORNING.

I SAID GOOD MORNING, MISS WATSON.

YES?

THAT MEANS YOU FOLLOW ME, NO?

IT DOES?

I SEE OTHER TITANS OF INDUSTRY DO STUFF LIKE THAT.

TITANS?

THEY STORM INTO THEIR EMPIRE AND PEOPLE JUST START FOLLOWING THEM, HANGING ON EVERY WORD, WRITING DOWN EVERYTHING THEY SAY AS IF--

I'VE BEEN WAITING HERE FOR FORTY MINUTES.

AM I LATE OR ARE YOU EARLY?

YOU'RE LATE.

I THOUGHT THAT MIGHT BE IT.

IT IS IT. FORTY MINUTES OF IT.

IT WAS WORTH A SHOT--

I'VE BEEN STARING AT THAT GIANT PICTURE OF YOUR FATHER FOR FORTY MINUTES.

OH, THAT'S NOT MY FATHER, THAT'S JUST THE MAN WHO RAISED ME.

WHAT?

(STORY FOR ANOTHER TIME.)

I'M SORRY I WAS LATE, AND THANK YOU FOR WAITING.

I WAS WONDERING IF YOU REMEMBERED OFFERING ME A JOB.

OF COURSE I DO.

AND YOU ARE?

ARE YOU SERIOUS RIGHT NOW?

NO.

WHAT I AM IS EMBARRASSED THAT I KEPT YOU WAITING, AND I WAS TRYING TO COVER IT UP WITH A JOKE THAT WASN'T ALL THAT FUNNY--

FORTY MINUTES.

IT WOULD ONLY BE FUNNY IF YOU, AND HALF THE ENGLISH-SPEAKING PEOPLE ON THIS PLANET, DIDN'T THINK OF ME AS BEING FLAKY AS A FRESH CROISSANT.

IT'S ONLY FUNNY IF IT'S NOT TRUE.

THAT IS TRUE.

WHICH PART?

CAN WE START OVER?

UM, ALL OF IT.

IT'S YOUR HOUSE AND YOUR DIME.

HI. I'M TONY STARK.

I'M A HOT MESS OF A HUMAN BEING AND I NEED YOU TO MAKE ME LESS SO.

WHICH MEANS...?

FOLLOW ME.

...HERE'S THE THING, AND I DON'T WANT YOU TO TAKE THIS IN ANY WAY, SHAPE, OR FORM *BADLY*, BUT I ALREADY HAD THIS CONVERSATION.

WITH WHO?

WITH YOU.

WHEN?

IN MY HEAD.

IT'S A PROBLEM I HAVE.

I KNEW YOU WERE GOING TO SAY THIS TO ME AND I KNEW WHAT I WOULD SAY IN RESPONSE.

LIKE A SUPER-POWER THING, OR--?

NO.

WELL, NOT REALLY.

I SEE CONVERSATIONS COMING DOWN THE STREET.

I KNEW YOU WERE GOING TO HIT ME WITH THIS AND I KNEW I WAS GOING TO AGREE WITH IT AND I WAS ALREADY ON TO OTHER THINGS WHILE WE WERE TALKING.

IT'S JUST HOW MY MIND WORKS.

IT'S REALLY HARD FOR HUMAN INTERACTIONS TO SURPRISE ME.

OKAY.

WHY WOULD YOU TELL ME THIS?

BECAUSE I WANT YOU TO UNDERSTAND WHAT YOU'RE DEALING WITH.

MY WHEELS TURN DIFFERENTLY THAN MOST OTHERS AND I WANT YOU TO--

DO YOU EXPECT ME TO NOW DO OR SAY

I CALLED PEPPER POTTS.

MOST PEOPLE

ADVANCED
ARTIFICIAL
INTELLIGENCE.

SHE'S NOT
REAL?

I HAVE IT ON PRETTY GOOD
AUTHORITY THAT I'M *MORE REAL*
THAN THE TWO OF YOU PUT
TOGETHER AND I'M DAMN
WELL GOING TO *OUTLAST*
YOU BOTH.

WE
CALL HER
FRIDAY.

NOT IF
I DON'T PAY THE
ELECTRIC BILL.

GOOD
THING I DO THAT
FOR YOU.

YES.

ARTIFICIAL
TELLIGENCE--

--SHOULD NOT
BE TALKING ABOUT
CONTROLLING THE
WORLD.

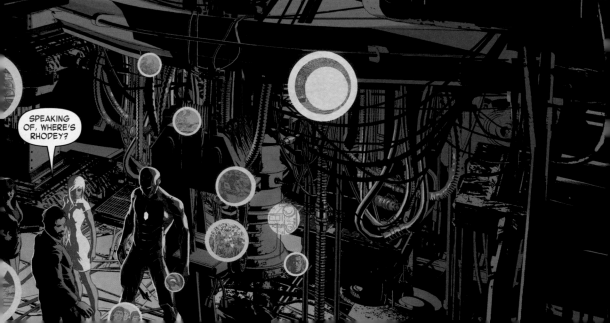

SPEAKING
OF, WHERE'S
RHODEY?

HE HAS NOT CALLED IN.

CALL HIM, THEN.

HE HASN'T ANSWERED.

WHERE IS HE?

TOKYO. WHERE YOU SENT HIM.

WHO'S RHODEY?

BEST FRIEND. JAMES RHODES. COLONEL. WAR MACHINE. HAS HIS OWN ARMOR.

OH, HIM. WHY IS HE IN TOKYO?

LOOKING INTO SOMETHING FOR ME.

WHICH, BY THE WAY, WAS ME DELEGATING RESPONSIBILITY SO I COULD BE HERE TO GO OVER THIS WITH YOU.

YOU WERE FORTY MINUTES LATE.

IMAGINE HOW LATE I'D BE IF I WAS IN TOKYO RIGHT NOW!

FRIDAY, CALL HIM AGAIN.

AND WHERE'S THE TRACKING DEVICE I PUT IN HIS ARMOR?

WHEN?

HE HAD IT REMOVED.

PROBABLY FIVE MINUTES AFTER YOU GAVE HIM THE ARMOR.

IT'S ALMOST LIKE HE DIDN'T CARE.

I'M GOING TO SUIT UP.

BUT IT WAS THERE SO I COULD TRACK HIM ON JUST SUCH AN OCCASION.

AND FLY TO TOKYO?

I SENT HIM ON A MISSION AND NOW HE'S MISSING. I *HAVE* TO GO.

NO. THAT'S WHAT YOU *SHOULD* DO, BUT HOW *LONG* WILL IT TAKE YOU TO GET TO TOKYO?

I'M FASTER THAN I LOOK.

NO, I MEAN: DO YOU KNOW ANYONE IN TOKYO WHO COULD HELP YOU *RIGHT NOW* WHILE YOU'RE ON YOUR WAY?

FRIDAY? ANYBODY FRIENDLY IN TOKYO?

THERE IS SOMEONE.

WHO?

YOU WON'T LOVE IT.

WHO?!

THEY ARE JUST VISITING.

WHO?!

PETER PARKER.

ALL RIGHT, CALL HIM.

YOU HAVE A PROBLEM WITH PETER PARKER?

ONLY THE FACT THAT HE'S DOING MY ACT DOWN TO THE TEE WHILE MY COMPANY IS BLEEDING DRY AND HIS IS ON THE RISE.

HIS COMPANY--

HE'S KICKING MY ASS.

HE'S NOT AVAILABLE.

HE WOULDN'T TAKE THE CALL?

HE WAS INDISPOSED.

DID YOU TELL HIM IT WAS KIND OF AN EMERGENCY?

I'LL CALL BACK.

ACTUALLY, USE THIS NUMBER. IT'S HIS EMERGENCY NUMBER.

YOU HAVE PETER PARKER'S EMERGENCY PRIVATE NUMBER?

YOU SAID IT WAS AN EMERGENCY.

WHY DO YOU HAVE PETER PARKER'S EMERGENCY PRIVATE NUMBER?

IT'S... COMPLICATED.

ARE YOU HIS BIOLOGICAL FATHER?

WHAT? NO.

TOKYO.

I'M LITERALLY SWINGING AROUND LOOKING FOR AN ARMORED MAN IN THE MOST DENSELY POPULATED PLACE ON THE PLANET.

GRANTED, IT'S A LOT LESS CROWDED UP HERE THAN DOWN THERE.

AND THIS ROOFTOP IS THE LAST PLACE THEY COULD TRACK HIM TO.

WHY DOESN'T HE HAVE A TRACKER IN THE ARMOR?

STARK PROBABLY *DID* PUT ONE IN THERE AND RHODEY TOOK IT OUT THE MINUTE TONY STARK LEFT THE ROOM.

THERE'S NOTHING HERE.

I'LL KEEP SWINGING AROUND, BUT...

HEY, HOW DID STARK GET MY PRIVATE EMERGENCY NUMBER?

BANG
CLANG

WHAT ARE YOU DOING IN THERE?

ZZZ/// CLANG

THUMP
THUMP
THUMP

WHAT *IS* SHE DOING IN THERE?

SHE SHOULDN'T EVEN *BE* HERE.

SHE'S, LIKE, ELEVEN YEARS OLD.

ANSWER THE DOOR!

WE *KNOW* YOU'RE IN THERE, RIRI!

WHAT DO YOU WANT? IT'S THREE O'CLOCK IN THE MORNING!

WHATEVER, DISNEY CHANNEL.

WHATEVER YOU'RE DOING IN THERE...DO IT *QUIETER.*

SLAM

YOU HAVE TO BE KIDDING ME.

KID'S A REAL PIECE OF WORK.

8

TOKYO

DEATH IS THE EASY WAY OUT. WE HAVE OTHER THINGS WE CAN DO.

I WOULD RETHINK THIS.

YOU'VE FOUGHT SO HARD IN YOUR LIFE.

YOU MUST KNOW WHICH FIGHTS YOU CAN WIN AND WHICH FIGHTS YOU CANNOT.

YUP.

PACK

DO NOT CHASE HIM.

I HAVE THIS.

A'RIGHT! COME ON! YOU WANNA SHOW ME SOMETHIN'? SHOW ME SOMETHIN'!

SKAASSHHH

HR!

SMACK

HA!

WHOA.

OKAY.

THAT WAS ALMOST SOMETHING.

DAMN YOU, AMERICAN.

FRIDAY CAN GIVE YOU THE TOUR, GET YOU SET UP WITH AN OFFICE...

PICK A GOOD ONE, YOU'LL BE LIVING IN IT.

AND YOU CAN WARM AND FUZZY YOURSELF TO THE NEW SURROUNDINGS 'TIL I GET BACK.

STARK.
HARES
NASDAQ:STRK)
LOSED DOWN
OR THE DAY
2%, SETTING
DISASTROUS
RESH MULTI-
EAR LOW.

"OKAY, SO, MARY JANE, I HAVE TO GO TO JAPAN AND FIND MY FRIEND."

HOURS AGO.

YOU'RE GOING TO, UM, LEAVE ME ALONE WITH THE--WITH HER?

SHE'S GREAT. SHE KNOWS WHERE EVERYTHING IS.

I DON'T EVEN KNOW WHERE THE BATHROOMS ARE.

WHERE DO YOU GO TO THE BATHROOM?

IN THE SUIT.

THAT'S THE ORIGINAL REASON I INVENTED IT.

KIDDING.

TANG

TONY STARK.

THIS DAY JUST BECAME SO INTERESTING.

HOW THE-- FRIDAY! OVERRIDE THIS! SHUT THIS DOWN!

I HAVE NO CONTROL OVER THIS.

CLEARLY.

I MEAN, THIS IS NOT A TECHNOLOGY THAT I HAVE ANY ACCESS TO OR CONTROL OVER.

IS IT MAGNETIC?

I COULD FIGHT THAT.

MAYBE THIS IS ONE OF THOSE-- UH-OH.

MY WEB-SHOOTERS!

THIS IS WHAT YOU'VE BEEN DEALING WITH ALL NIGHT?

HAVE I NOT SAID THANK YOU FOR THIS EXPERIENCE?

WE'LL DISCUSS THE BOXERS LATER.

NO, WE WON'T.

WE'VE NEVER COME ACROSS A SYSTEM INTERFACE LIKE THIS.

SHE'S USING TWO OF MY ARMORS TO BEAT MY ASS.

I KNOW YOU HATE THIS, BUT I RECOMMEND RETREAT.

I HAVE CALLED THE OTHER AVENGERS, BUT THEY ARE--

HALF A WORLD AWAY.

I'M WORRIED ABOUT THE SAFETY OF LOCAL AUTHORITIES IF WE CALL THEM TO BACK--

YOU'RE RIGHT, DON'T CALL LOCAL AUTHORITIES.

WHO IS SHE AND HOW IS SHE DOING THIS?

TAIKYAKU SHIRO!

I WILL END THIS MYSELF.

UM...

GUYS, RUN.

TONY--

I SEE IT.

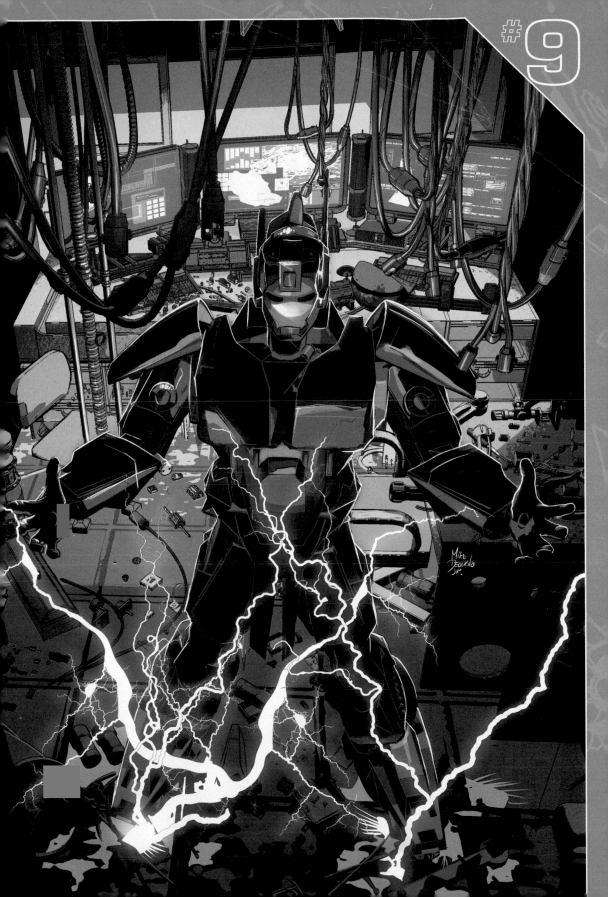

9

STARK
IN COMPANY NEWS, STARK (STRK) SHARES FELL TO A NEARLY 15-MONTH LOW AFTER TONY STARK WAS A NO-SHOW FOR THE QUARTERLY INVESTORS' CALL.

WHERE IS TONY STARK?

I'M SORRY, MISTER LYNCH.

DID YOU HAVE AN APPOINTMENT?

I DON'T *NEED* AN APPOINTMENT, FRIDAY.

I'M A MAJOR STOCKHOLDER IN THIS HOUSE OF CARDS.

WHERE IS *TONY STARK?*

I PROMISE YOU, MR. LYNCH, I WILL FORWARD ANY MESSAGES.

BECAUSE I HAVE IT ON

HE WAS LAST CHARTED OVER THE SKIES OF OSAKA... *FOUR WEEKS AGO.*

AND NO ONE HAS SEEN OR HEARD FROM HIM SINCE.

I WILL FORWARD YOUR MESS--

AND IT GOT ME THINKING--

--HOW LONG UNTIL THIS CORPORATION CALLS IT?

I KNOW HE'S A BIG-TIME SUPER HERO AND HAS A HABIT OF GOING OFF INTO SPACE FOR "LONG VACATIONS"...

...BUT WHEN HE DOES THAT, HE FILES IT WITH THE BOARD.

THIS, IT SEEMS, IS DIFFERENT.

IF HE IS NOT HERE...IS HE IN ANOTHER DIMENSION?

IN SPACE?

IS HE DEAD?

BECAUSE THIS COMPANY HAS PROTOCOLS.

HIS ESTATE HAS PROTOCOLS.

AND IF TONY STARK IS NO LONGER WITH US,

HOLY @#$@#, RIRI!

DID--DID YOU MAKE THIS YOURSELF?

AT FIRST I DID IT AS A DARE--

WHO DARED YOU?

I DARED MYSELF.

RIRI, WHERE'D YOU GET THE PARTS?

I MADE THEM.

YOU MADE THEM *FROM* SOMETHING.

THINGS THAT BELONGED TO *OTHER PEOPLE* AROUND CAMPUS?

JUST, YOU KNOW, THINGS I FOUND AROUND CAMPUS.

I DON'T FOLLOW. SUPPOSED TO *WHAT*?

MY POINT IS, NOW...NOW I THINK I WAS *SUPPOSED* TO DO IT.

I DID WHAT I DID, DIDN'T KNOW WHY I WAS DOING IT, AND NOW THERE'S ALL THIS ONLINE CHATTER THAT *TONY STARK* IS MISSING.

MAYBE DEAD.

MISSING?

GEEZ.

NO ONE HAS *SEEN* THE DUDE.

WHERE IS TONY STARK?
THE WORST IS FEARED

AND YOU THINK YOU'RE SUPPOSED TO *WHAT*--?

AM I CRAZY?

OH, YOU'RE THE CRAZIEST.

GIRL, FIRST OF ALL, YOU'RE FIFTEEN YEARS OLD.

WHAT DOES *THAT* HAVE TO DO WITH ANYTHING?

YOU MADE THIS OUT OF THINGS YOU STOLE FROM THE CAMPUS AND NOW YOU THINK YOU'RE SUPPOSED TO BE THE NEW--

COME ON, YOU DON'T SEE THE CONNECTION?

DOES IT WORK?

KNOCK KNOCK

RIRI WILLIAMS?

UH-OH. YES?

THIS IS THE HEAD OF CAMPUS SECURITY.

MAY I PLEASE SPEAK WITH YOU?

UM...I'M NOT DRESSED.

WHAT IS GOING ON?

PLEASE OPEN THE DOOR, MISS WILLIAMS.

WHAT IS THIS ABOUT?

WELL, ON TOP OF YOU NOT ATTENDING CLASS FOR THE LAST COUPLE OF DAYS AND THE REPEATED NOISE COMPLAINTS FROM YOUR FELLOW DORM MATES...

...WE HAVE SOME CONCERNING SECURITY FOOTAGE WE'D LIKE TO DISCUSS WITH YOU.

SECURITY FOOTAGE?

WERE YOU IN THE ROBOTICS LAB TWO NIGHTS AGO?

UH, HOLD ON.

MISS WILLIAMS?

AND SHE'S HERE ON SCHOLARSHIP.

MISS WILLIAMS?

YOU HAVE THE KEY, OPEN THE DOOR.

WE'RE--WE'RE COMING IN, MISS WILLIAMS.

DO YOU KNOW THE JEOPARDY IN WHICH YOU HAVE PUT YOUR ACADEMIC...

...CAREER?

YEAH, I FIGURED

OSAKA.

THUMP

THUMP
THUMP
THUMP

EXCUSE ME!

YOU'RE NOT GOING TO START ANY TROUBLE...

...ARE YOU?

OH, NO.

YUKIO, LAST CHANCE.

WHERE IS HE?

COLONEL RHODES, THIS ISN'T FAIR.

I DO NOT KNOW WHERE TONY STARK IS. NO ONE KNOWS--

SEE, YUKIO, THE WAY I SEE IT IS WE HELP EACH OTHER.

YOU GET TO DO WHATEVER YOU DO HERE, A EVERY ONCE IN A WHILE YOU HELP ME.

YOU STOP HELPING ME? I START LOSING INTEREST IN HELPING YOU.

I PROMISE YOU...I--I HAVE MY EAR TO THE GROUND.

WHERE IS HE?

I THINK-- HONESTLY, I THINK HE'S DEAD.

I'M SORRY.

THIS IS RHODES.

THE WORD IS GIVEN.

SHUT IT DOWN.

NO.

<NOBODY MOVE!>*

<YOU ARE ALL UNDER ARREST!>

<THIS ESTABLISHMENT IS NOW SEIZED!>

<HEY!>

*RANSLATED OM JAPANESE.

LAST CHANCE. ACTUALLY, LAST CHANCE WAS THIRTY SECONDS AGO.

BUT THIS IS THE ONLY WAY YOUR ASS DOESN'T GET ROLLED INTO A JAPANESE PRISON TONIGHT.

WHICH I HEAR ARE THE BEST PRISONS.

<CALM DOWN!>

<PLEASE, I-- I JUST WORK HERE!>

WHERE IS MY FRIEND?

WHERE IS TONY STARK?

AND LOOK WHO'S HERE.

BIOHACK NINJAS.

NOW *WHAT* WOULD THEY BE DOING HERE?

<PUT DOWN THE-- *AGGH!*>

NO PROBLEM.

REMOTE CONTROL ENGAGE.

TK

OKAY, NINJAS, *DON'T* RUN FROM MY SCARY ARMOR.

STUN PELLETS IT IS.

KACHUNK
KACHUNK
KACHUNK
KACHUNK

AAAGGH!

KACHUNK
KACHUNK

HO!

SMAASSHH

DUDE, I'M KIND OF IN THE MIDDLE OF SOMETHING!

DUDE, YOU'RE REALLY STARTING TO PISS ME OFF!

AGGH!

SMAACCKKK

I ASSUME YOU DON'T WANT TO BE HERE ANYMORE, MISS YUKIO.

WHO ARE YOU?

JUST A GRATEFUL CUSTOMER.

NO!
<CLOSE THE DOORS!>

NO, DON'T LET THEM GET AWAY!

SMASCCKK

AGH!

I'M SORRY I SCARED YOU.

I CAN BE THEATRICAL. I FORGET THAT.

PLEASE, CALL ME VICTOR.

HOW DID YOU EVEN GET IN HERE? THI--THIS IS A SECURE FACILITY.

I'M SURE IT IS.

BUT I AM A MASTER OF THE MYSTIC ARTS AS WELL AS YOUR PEER AND COLLEAGUE IN THE "PHYSICAL" SCIENCES.

WHAT DOES THAT MEAN?

I OPENED THE DOOR...WITH A SPELL.

A SPELL? A LITTLE MAGIC.

GET OUT OF HERE.

I'M SORRY IF I STARTLED YOU.

NO. IT'S JUST THAT DOCTOR DOOM JUST WALTZED INTO MY LAB.

YOU ROMANTICALLY CONNECTED YOURSELF TO TONY STARK...YOU CHOSE TO RUN IN THESE CIRCLES.

WHAT?

IF YOU'RE GOING TO BE WITH TONY STARK, YOU ARE GOING TO FIND YOURSELF TALKING TO COLORFUL CHARACTERS OF ALL--

GET OUT!

HAVE YOU SEEN HIM?

FOUR WEEKS IS A LONG TIME TO BE MISSING.

HAVE YOU HEARD FROM HIM?

IT'S OKAY TO BE WORRIED.

NO.

NOW LEAVE.

WHAT DO YOU WANT, DOOM?

I TOLD YOU. I AM LOOKING FOR--

WHAT DO YOU WANT FROM *HIM*?

HUMAN TESTING.

IF YOU HAVE THE CURE FOR ALZHEIMER'S IN YOUR GRASP AND YOU DON'T GO TO HUMAN TESTING IMMEDIATELY, YOU ARE FAILING--

WHY DON'T *YOU* USE YOUR MAGIC TO CURE IT?

I'M SORRY?

YOU KNOW EVERYTHING.

YOU KNOW WHAT EVERYONE ELSE SHOULD BE DOING.

YOU SAY YOU WANT THIS BIG SECOND CHANCE IN LIFE.

DO SOMETHING THAT HELPS HUMANITY THAT'S AS BOLD AS THE THINGS YOU WERE DOING WHEN YOU WERE TRYING TO DESTROY HUMANITY.

SEE? I WAS NEVER TRYING TO ACTIVELY *DESTROY* HUMANITY--

--I WAS TRYING TO *RULE* IT, WHICH--

NO, I SEE YOUR POINT.

BUT

WHAT KIND OF COST?

IF YOU USE THIS MYSTIC ENERGY *TOO MUCH*...

...SAY THE AMOUNT OF ENERGY ONE WOULD NEED TO CURE SOMETHING, TO CHANGE SOMETHING, *THAT BIG*...

...IT'S NOT HARD TO IMAGINE THE COST WOULD BE *ENORMOUS*.

AND AFTER ALL *I'VE* SEEN ON THIS PLANE, AND OTHERS, I AM NOT WILLING TO TAKE THE CHANCE OF BRINGING SOMETHING HERE THAT IS WORSE THAN THE CURSE YOU ARE TRYING TO CURE.

YOU PROMISE ME YOU DON'T KNOW WHERE TONY IS.

WHY WOULD I COME HERE TO ASK YOU IF I DID?

BUT ONE COULD ONLY IMAGINE...

WHAT?

THE LIFE OF AN ADVENTURER, AN AVENGER, A KNIGHT IS, BY PERCENTAGES, A SHORTER ONE.

PLEASE. LEAVE.

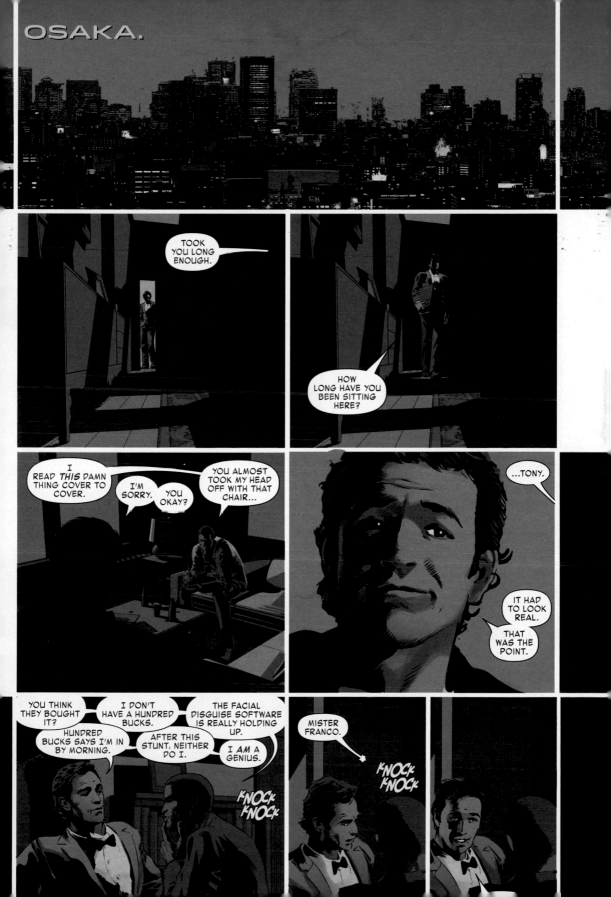

OSAKA.

OSAKA. NOW.

@#$@#$!

@#$@#!

COLONEL JAMES RHODES, A.K.A. WAR MACHINE.

TONY STARK, A.K.A. IRON MAN.

HE'S DISGUISING HIMSELF USING ADVANCED BIOTECHNOLOGY. REALLY.

MISTER FRANCO?

KNOCK

WHAT DO WE DO?

"WE"?

WE DO NOTHING. YOU LEAVE.

THIS IS IT.

THIS IS WHAT WE'VE BEEN WAITING FOR.

SMAASSHH

@#$@#$!

SMAASSSHH

UM...

I AM ZHANG.

UM... OKAY.

WHY DIDN'T YOU ANSWER YOUR DOOR?

I THOUGHT YOU WERE MY LANDLORD.

YOU WILL COME WITH ME NOW.

YOUR ENGLISH IS VERY GOOD, BUT IF YOU'RE TRYING TO ASK ME OUT, THE PROPER WORDING IS--

NO. YOU WILL COME WITH ME.

NO, I GOT

YOU WILL COME WITH ME.

YOU WILL PUT THIS ON.

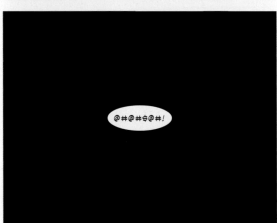

MAN, THIS IS SOME WEIRD @#$@#.

I CAN *HEAR* YOU, YOU KNOW.

I HEAR YOU WALKING AROUND AND WHISPERING IN JAPANESE...

...WHICH I *UNDERSTAND*, BY THE WAY.

MOSTLY.

OH, MAN. IF THIS IS ONE OF THOSE WEIRD JAPANESE GAME SHOWS WHERE THEY SHAVE MY SACK OR SOMETHING...I SWEAR TO GOD!

I--I AM GOING TO SUE YOU IN--IN--IN WORLD COURT!

I MEAN, IF YOU'RE GOING TO--OH.

WHEW.

GOD! THAT THING *STUNK*.

HOW DO YOU KNOW ME?

THE YUKIO CLUB.

OH, HEY, I--I WAS JUST--

YOU WERE A GREAT HELP TO FRIENDS OF OURS.

YOU READ MY FILE?

THAT'S A BLACK FILE.

THAT'S-- HOW DID YOU GET ACCESS TO A S.H.I.E.L.D. BLACK FILE?

THIS IS MARY JANE WATSON CALLING.

OH, REALLY? HE'S *STILL* OUT?

OKAY, FINE. YES, HE KNOWS THE *UMBER*.

HE *USED* TO BE MY AGENT.

NEW YORK BULLETIN

STARK ASSETS UNDER SIEGE

HEYYO!

AW, MAN, THAT'S COOL.

I DIDN'T KNOW HE WAS REAL.

WHAT?

WHAT THE HELL?

UH-OH.

HELLO, MISS WATSON.

FRIDAY!

HOW--HOW DID YOU GET IN HERE?

YOU LET ME IN WHEN YOU CONNECTED THE SERVER.

WHEN DID I DO THAT?

WHEN YOU PRESSED THE BUTTON.

YOU TOLD ME TO PRESS THE BUTTON. I ASKED.

WHAT? WHAT IS THIS?

YOU ARE DESPERATELY NEEDED BACK AT STARK HEADQUARTERS.

NO! I--I--I DIDN'T ACCEPT THE JOB.

I'M NOT INTERESTED.

MISS WATSON... STARK INDUSTRIES

THE COMPANY IS UNDER SIEGE BY THE STARK BOARD OF DIRECTORS.

THEY ARE MEETING, RIGHT NOW, AND PLANNING TO "UNPLUG" ME AND SEIZE CONTROL OF THE COMPANY.

I'M--I'M SORRY TO HEAR THAT, BUT--WHY AM I TALKING TO YOU?

I AM AN ARTIFICIAL INTELLIGENCE. I AM FAR MORE THAN A COMPUTER PROGRAM.

YOU'RE A COMPUTER PROGRAM!

WHERE'S TONY STARK?

IF--IF THE RUMORS ARE TRUE... IF HE IS DEAD, THEN ISN'T THE BOARD RIGHT IN THEIR--

HE'S NOT DEAD.

WHERE IS HE?

FRIDAY? WHERE IS HE?

WHAT'S MORE IMPORTANT THAN SAVING THE COMPANY THAT HE SPENT HIS ENTIRE LIFE BUILDING?

SHOW ME.

SHOW ME WHAT AN AMERICAN NAVY SEAL TURNED BLACK-OPS S.H.I.E.L.D. AGENT CAN DO.

WHAT, LIKE HOW MANY PUSH-UPS OR--

OH.

SORRY ABOUT THE ARM.

BUT I'M KEEPING THIS.

GLOWING LASER SWORD. NICE.

I WOULD HAVE KILLED FOR ONE OF THESE WHEN I WAS TEN.

NOW, ARE YOU GOING TO TELL ME WHAT THIS IS OR AM I GOING TO SLICE MY WAY OUT OF HERE AND--

DO YOU KNOW OF THE TERRIGEN?

I KNOW THE WORD.

THE TERRIGEN CLOUD.

OH, YEAH.

THE INHUMANS.

IT WOULD SEEM THAT I AM ONE OF THEM.

I WAS A YOUNG WOMAN OF RELATIVELY LITTLE CONSEQUENCE, BUT I HAVE BEEN REBORN.

I HAVE THE POWER TO CONTROL LIVE TECHNOLOGY.

AND IN THIS WORLD, THAT IS QUITE USEFUL.

OH, YEAH?

CO-- OH!

AND WITH THAT POWER CAME THE CHANCE TO SEND HYDRA AND A.I.M. AND THE BROTHERHOOD OF MUTANTS AND EVERYONE ELSE WHO HAS PREYED ON THIS LAND BACK TO WHERE THEY CAME FROM.

AWAY.

IF YOU HAVE TECHNOLOGY, I CAN TAKE IT FROM YOU, I CAN MAKE IT PART OF MYSELF...FOR A TIME.

IT WAS I WHO KILLED TONY STARK.

WITH HIS OWN ARMOR.

SO YOU'RE THE TECHNO GOLEM.

AND WITH STARK'S DEMISE AND WITH OUR CONTROL OF THIS PART OF THE WORLD SECURE...IT IS TIME TO REACH OUT.

REACH OUT TO...?

AMERICA. S.H.I.E.L.D. HYDRA. WAKANDA. ATLANTIS. ATTILAN.

AMBITIOUS.

BUT WHY AM I HERE?

A MAN OF YOUR TALENTS, HIDING IN THE SHADOWS, AS FAR AWAY FROM THE WORLD THAT BIRTHED HIM, IS VERY INTERESTING TO ME.

IT IS WHERE MANY OF OUR GROWING CLAN HAVE COME FROM...

I WANT YOU TO FIND AND KILL JAMES RHODES.

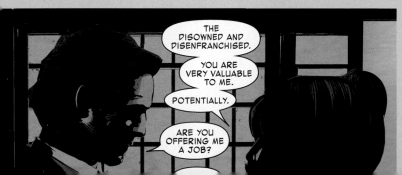

THE DISOWNED AND DISENFRANCHISED.

YOU ARE VERY VALUABLE TO ME.

POTENTIALLY.

ARE YOU OFFERING ME A JOB?

HEY, SHARON?

HEY!

RIRI?

ARE YOU ON A PLANE? YOU SOUND LIKE YOU'RE ON A--

I NEED TO ASK YOU A QUESTION.

WHERE ARE YOU?

MAIDEN VOYAGE.

WHAT

WHAT?

WHOO!

IF IRON MAN WAS A WOMAN, WHAT WOULD YOU CALL HIM?

IRON LADY?

IRON WOMAN?

NO.

I COULD THINK OF T MYSELF.

234.5

6.9 PSI

RIRI?

STARK HEADQUARTERS.

IN COMPANY NEWS, STARK (STRK) SHARES FELL AGAIN AMIDST RUMORS THAT THE BOARD OF DIRECTORS IS CONSIDERING A MUTINY AGAINST TONY STARK, AS HE WAS A NO-SHOW FOR THE QUARTERLY INVESTOR'S CALL.

CAN I HELP YOU, MR. LYNCH?

IS THAT HER?

IGNORE HER. FRIDAY'S NOT REAL.

SHE LOOKS REAL.

SHE'S A HOLOGRAM OF AN ARTIFICIAL INTELLIGENCE.

AND SHE'S BEEN RUNNING STARK INDUSTRIES?

IT.

MISTER LYNCH, I ASSURE YOU MY PROGRAMMING IS SECURE AND OPERATIONAL.

NO! STOP TALKING TO ME.

YOU'RE THE FIRST THING WE'RE UNPLUGGING.

YOU DO NOT HAVE THE AUTHORITY--

WELL, THE BOARD VOTED. IT'S DONE.

TONY STARK IS MISSING AND PRESUMED DEAD BY ANY DEFINITION OF THE LAW.

WE ARE TAKING CONTROL OF THE COMPANY.

THIS IS THE GHOST. WE HAVE CONTRACTED HIS SPECIAL SKILLS TO BREAK INTO THE LAB AND TO OVERRIDE THE SECURE SERVERS.

YOU CAN OPEN THEM FOR US OR WE WILL TAKE CARE OF IT OURSELVES.

I APPRECIATE THAT.

GHOST.

EARN YOUR MONEY.

BREAKING INTO TONY STARK'S LAB?

WITH PERMISSION?

HONESTLY, I WOULD HAVE DONE THIS FOR FREE.

AGAIN, I MUST INSIST THAT YOU RESPECT TONY STARK'S WISHES AND ALLOW--

JUST DO IT.

IF YOU'LL EXCUSE ME.

THAT WAS WEIRD.

UM...

WHAT? IS HE IN THERE?

IS HE DEAD IN THERE?

WHAT EXACTLY DID YOU EXPECT TO FIND IN HERE?

OH.

OSAKA, JAPAN.

KUMAMOTO NORTH POLICE STATION, KUMAMOTO PREFECTURE.

HE IS HERE?

THE AMERICAN WAR MACHINE IS BACK.

COLONEL JAMES RHODES.

HE MUST KNOW SOMETHING.

HE IS NOT THE ONLY ONE, TOMOE.

I'M SORRY.

THE LADY THOR HAS BEEN SPOTTED.

WHERE?

IN DOWNTOWN OSAKA.

THOR *AND* WAR MACHINE ARE *BOTH* HERE?

SEE, ZHANG, IT IS HAPPENING.

THEY ARE LOOKING FOR STARK.

THEY ARE LOOKING FOR *US.* IN RETALIATION FOR STARK.

THIS-- THESE ARE THE *SAME* MISTAKES THAT *THE HAND* AND *HYDRA* AND *SO MANY OTHERS* HAVE MADE OVER AND OVER.

SLOPPY MISTAKES THAT BRING THESE AMERICAN AVENGERS *RIGHT* TO OUR DOORSTEP.

WE WERE PAINFULLY UNSUCCESSFUL IN HUNTING DOWN JAMES RHODES BEFORE HE ESCAPED OUR COUNTRY.

WE COULDN'T GET *NEAR* THAT GALLIVANTING SPIDER-MAN.

WE LOST OUR MOST VALUED ASSET... ANONYMITY.

ALL OF THIS BECAUSE OF THAT *DAMNED MADAME MASQUE.*

WHAT NOW, TOMOE?

I CAN HAVE THE BIOHACK NINJAS POWER DOWN AND DROP OUT OF SIGHT UNTIL THIS ALL BLOWS OVER.

I THINK RIGHT NOW SURVIVAL TRUMPS EGO.

AND WHEN WORD GETS OUT THAT WE HID FROM THE AMERICAN HEROES?

WHERE IS OUR NEW RECRUIT?

WHERE IS OUR EX-S.H.I.E.L.D. AGENT, FRANCO?

HAVE WE HEARD FROM HIM?

NOT SINCE YOU SENT HIM TO TRACK DOWN JAMES RHODES FOR US.

WELL... THAT IS HARDLY NECESSARY NOW.

YOU CAN TAKE HIM, YOU KNOW.

WHO?

THE AMERICAN WAR MACHINE.

MAYBE. BUT THOR...

...IS ANOTHER SITUATION ENTIRELY.

ENTIRELY.

WHAT SAY YOU, TOMOE?

DAMN IT!

GLACK

HEY, DID YOU TRY THE COFFEE?

IT'S INSANE.

RHODEY?

WHAT ARE YOU *DOING* HERE?

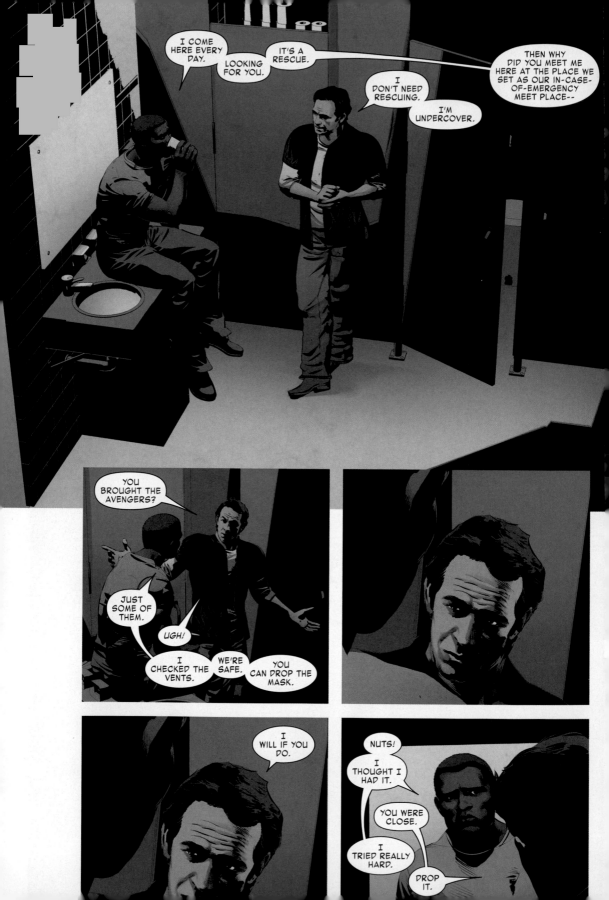

DON'T SWEAT IT, MS. MARVEL.

RHODEY'S MY OLDEST, BESTEST FRIEND.

AND I'VE LIVED THROUGH A SKRULL INVASION OR TWO IN MY TIME.

OKAY, WELL, I'M AN INHUMAN SHAPE-SHIFTER, I KNOW HOW I MAKE MY FACE DO WHAT IT DOES.

HOW ARE YOU DOING THAT?

UGH, THAT FEELS SO MUCH BETTER.

YOU'RE DOING THAT WITH TECH?

OH, MAN.

BIOTECH, ACTUALLY.

THAT FEELS GOOD.

M'ITCHY.

I'M TRYING TO THINK OF A POLITER WAY TO SAY THIS BUT: YOU'RE NUTS, MISTER STARK.

YEAH.

SO, WHY ARE YOU HERE?

RHODEY BROUGHT US ALL HERE.

AND HE PROMISED I'D BE BACK BY 6 P.M. JERSEY TIME.

AND HE WANTS YOU TO KNOW, AND I QUOTE: "I'M NOT GOING TO SAY SORRY FOR THIS."

SORRY FOR WHAT?

I HAVE HIM.

"WHAT DID YOU JUST DO?"

THAT'S NOT HER.

NO, IT IS.

IT'S--

THAT'S THE *OTHER* ONE.

THAT'S ZHANG.

SHE WAS--

TOMOE IS YOUNGER.

THAT IS ZHANG, TOMOE'S RIGHT-HAND LADY PERSON.

TO BE FAIR--

YOU GOT THE WRONG ASIAN WOMAN.

TO BE FAIR, WHEN WE FOUGHT HER, IT WAS DARK. IT WAS WEEKS AGO...

NO ONE IS ACCUSING YOU OF BEING RACIST.

THERE WERE A LOT OF-- *RACIST?* WHO SAID *RACIST?*

NO ONE.

THERE WERE A LOT OF GLOWING SWORDS AND SHE STOLE OUR ARMOR.

STOP. KICK YOURSELF LATER.

THIS TOMOE IS OUT THERE

WAIT. DID ANYONE--DID ANY OF YOU GIVE UP MY SECRET IDENTITY?

YOU HAVE A SECRET IDENTITY?

I THOUGHT EVERYONE KNEW

I HAVE RIGHTS!

SO DO THOSE WHO YOUR KIND EXPLOITS.

YOU. FRANCO!

YOU-- YOU SOLD US OUT!

I WAS JUST ABOUT TO SAY THE SAME TO YOU.

DEAR GOD...

THESE MONSTERS.

THEY GET EVERYBODY?

NO. NOT EVEN CLOSE. BUT ENOUGH.

AT LEAST TELL ME TOMOE IS COMING TO RESCUE US.

BECAUSE, AGH, I HAVE A SURPRISINGLY LOW THRESHOLD FOR PAIN.

YOU DON'T KNOW IF THEY GOT HER OR YOU DON'T KNOW WHEN SHE'S COMING TO RESCUE US?

I-- I DON'T KNOW.

SHE DISAPPEARED.

SHE TOLD US ONE PLAN BUT THEN THE AVENGERS WERE THERE INSTEAD.

ALMOST--

ALMOST WHAT?

ALMOST AS IF SHE KNEW THEY WERE COMING.

SHE BETRAYED US.

I HOPE I'M WRONG, BUT THIS FEELS--

--IT FEELS LIKE BETRAYAL.

AND THE FACT THAT I DON'T KNOW SCARES THE CRAP OUT OF ME.

AND I REALLY DIDN'T NEED RESCUING.

YES, YOU DID.

YOU ARE *NOT* AN AGENT OF S.H.I.E.L.D.

YOU ARE *NOT* INTELLIGENCE OR COUNTER-INTELLIGENCE.

YOU ARE A SUPER HERO AND YOU ARE A TITAN OF INDUSTRY.

YOU WERE USING THIS AS AN EXCUSE TO HIDE FROM YOUR LIFE.

I LOVE YOU.

BUT THAT WAS KIND OF MEAN.

WHAT IF THIS TECHNO GOLEM SHOWS UP ON MY FRONT DOOR?

SHE WON'T.

YOU DON'T KNOW THAT.

SURE, I DO.

BECAUSE

WE DID SHUT THESE BIOHACK NINJAS DOWN.

HERE WE GO...

BUT--

I STILL DON'T KNOW WHAT MADAME MASQUE STOLE FROM ME AND WHY THEY WANTED IT SO BADLY THAT THEY CAME OUT OF HIDING AND REVEALED THEMSELVES.

I LOVE YOU, TOO.

BUT IT WAS KIND OF TRUE.

IT WAS BOTH.

YOU HAVE TO GO BACK TO YOUR LIFE AND TELL EVERYONE YOU'RE STILL ALIVE.

S.H.I.E.L.D. IS ALREADY PUTTING TOGETHER ONE OF THEIR FANCY DEEP COVER TEAMS TO GO FIND THIS NEW INHUMAN THREAT.

OH, YOU.

HEY, FRIDAY.

MISS ME?

OH, HEY, I KNOW THE VOICE.

GIVE ME A HINT.

COULD YOU GET DR. AMARA ON THE PHONE AND SEE IF SHE STILL LIKES ME?

SURE.

HEY, DID YOU KNOW THERE'S A TEENAGER FLYING AROUND THE COUNTRY IN NEW ADVANCED ARMOR TECH?

UH, WHAT?

#9 AGE OF APOCALYPSE VARIANT BY CHRIS TURCOTTE